Uttering the Holy

Other Books by Adam Hughes

Petrichor, NYQ Books, 2010

Uttering the Holy

Adam Hughes

The New York Quarterly Foundation, Inc.
New York, New York

NYQ Books™ is an imprint of The New York Quarterly Foundation, Inc.

The New York Quarterly Foundation, Inc.
P. O. Box 2015
Old Chelsea Station
New York, NY 10113

www.nyqbooks.org

Copyright © 2012 by Adam Hughes

All rights reserved. No part of this book may be used or reproduced in any manner whatsoever without written permission of the author except in the case of brief quotations embodied in critical articles and reviews.

First Edition

Set in New Baskerville

Layout and Design by Raymond P. Hammond

Cover Photo ©2011 Steve Thompson | Thompson Creative Services
www.facebook.com/thompsoncreative

Author Photo Courtesy of Amy Clark Studios | www.amyclarkstudios.com

Library of Congress Control Number: 2012933646

ISBN: 978-1-935520-61-0

Uttering the Holy

Acknowledgments

"An Ant Contemplates the Suddenness of Death" first appeared in the Summer 2011 issue of the *Boston Literary Magazine.*

"Dead Sunflowers" first appeared in the *Barnwood International Poetry Magazine* in Winter 2011.

"En Ascuas es el Amor" first appeared in the Fall 2010 issue of the *Ante Review.*

"The Hill Gods" and "St. Brendan Sails to the Moon" appeared in the anthology *Tipping the Sacred Cow* (Fortunate Childe Press, 2011).

"Love Poem" first appeared in the August 2011 issue of *Pedestal Magazine.* "Vision Quests Terminate in Passages from the Farmer's Almanac" first appeared in *Pedestal's* October 2010 issue.

"A Pre-Elegy for Margaret" first appeared in issue 5 of the *Rufous City Review* in December 2011.

"Upon Exiting the Highway and Entering a Small Town in Southern Ohio" first appeared in the April 2011 issue of *Pirene's Fountain.*

"Variation on a Theme by God" appeared in *Ancient Paths.*

"Variations on a Theme by the Prophet Joel" first appeared in the Winter 2011 issue of *Rock and Sling.*

for Ellie

Contents

Prologue

Responsorial Ars Poetica / 17

Deep Calleth Unto Deep

The Art of Decay and Time-Lapse Photography / 21
Psalm / 22
Perichoresis / 24
On the Eighteenth of January it Rained in Central Ohio Because the Temperature was Forty-Three Degrees Fahrenheit / 25
Circadian / 26
Speleosis / 28
Forty Minutes Before Composing an Aubade / 29

Variations on a Theme by God

My Daughter Changes Her Mind About Shadows / 33
A Pre-Elegy for Margaret / 34
An Elegy for Margaret / 35
The Silence Between Words Can be as Beautiful as all the Gilded Syllables That Stand Out Like Stars Among the Blackgaps of Space / 36
Learning to Speak / 37
On Being Hugged by a Four-Year-Old Stranger / 38
Variation on a Theme by God / 39

Thought After Setting Oneself on Fire

Worth / 43
Sati / 44
Beneath McNamara's Window / 45
Alice Hertz / 46
being the final thoughts of Alfredo Ormando, on fire outside of St. Peter's Basilica protesting the Vatican's condemnation of homosexual Christians / 47
Wax / 48
In Remembrance / 49

To Taste the Feet of Bees

An Ant Contemplates the Suddenness of Death / 53
In Praise of Nomadism / 54
Rabbit / 55
Bee Stings / 56
Maneaters / 57
Meditation on the Dried and Severed Back Leg of a Grasshopper / 58
Dead Sunflowers / 59

Until Our Arms are Masts and Our Songs are Sails

Thresholds / 63
Inter-Oceanic Love Song / 64
Amelia / 66
Atoll / 67
for Mal / 67
A Glossary of Nautical Terms / 68
St. Brendan Sails to the Moon / 70
Parts Left Over After Translating Dichotomy / 72

Cell Phone Pictures of the Inside of My Pocket

Similes Written for Accompaniment on the Hurdy Gurdy / 77
Red / 78
Cell Phone Pictures of the Inside of My Pocket / 79
An Instruction Manual for Flight / 80
D.B. Cooper Dreams of Falling and Wakes to the Taste of River Stone Behind His Uvula / 82
D.B. Gives Instructions on Falling / 83
Upon Exiting the Highway and Entering a Town in Southern Ohio / 84

Arpeggios of Defiance

Address to the Nation / 87
In Anticipation of the Anniversary of a Death / 88
Prayer at the Birth of a Nation / 89
To an Artist with Broken Hands / 90
Elegy on a McDonald's Sign / 91
Upon Hearing of the Death of Osama Bin Laden / 92
The Gentler Tortures / 93

Of Love and Limerance

Love Poem / 97
Uttering the Holy / 98
We're Kings Among Runaways / 100
Post Coitum Omne Animal Triste Est / 101
On Dreaming of the Future / 102
Adiaphora / 104
Lines in Praise of Pacing / 105

Beneath the Burning

Vision Quests Terminate in Passages from the Farmer's Almanac / *111*
Kairos Hymn Fragments / *112*
Travelogue / *114*
After Certain Latin American Poets / *116*
Beneath the Orca Sky / *117*
Streetcorner Parousia / *118*
Another Rainy Day Poem / *119*

Echolocations of Prayer

The Glory of God is Man Fully Alive / *123*
For Ramadan: Dawn and Sunset / *124*
The Hill Gods / *125*
As I Went Down to the River to Pray / *126*
A Word to St. Damien of Molokai on the Occasion of His Canonization / *127*
Variations on a Theme by the Prophet Joel / *128*
Prayer to St. Margaret of Cortona / *129*

Epilogue

En Ascuas es el Amor / *133*

P. S.

When All Endings Look the Same / *139*

"To be a poet in a destitute time means: to attend, singing to the trace of the fugitive gods. This is why the poet, in the time of the world's night, utters the holy."

—Martin Heidegger

Prologue

Responsorial Ars Poetica

> *"I have read the poets in this issue, and for the most part, I think a LOT of my poetry is better."*
> —a scorned poet on an editor's Facebook page

I don't write good
poems—I write
tiny puffs
of grass-caught
clouds. They mock
with the coughs
of jays and bounce
from blade to blade
humming the tune
of a tuna
net. But they get caught
on dawn-leaked blades
and I can think of nothing
better.

Deep Calleth Unto Deep
―――――――――――――――――――――――――――

The Art of Decay and Time-Lapse Photography

See how the edges get eaten away
like snowflakes, moth-nibbled children's crafts
folded and cut until frozen and hanging
from the ceiling with fishing line? Time pauses
when you least want it to, blurring the falling shards
and smelling of old books. Soon the detritus
grows, whole sections sliding off like the fingertips
of a glacier. Before the end of the frame, the colors
blend into a dull grey, the result of mixing
all your Easter egg dyes. Everything happens so smoothly,

yet the results are so jagged. I've seen people fall
when they thought no one was looking; I carry those scenes
and watch them again when sitting at stoplights.
Of course the end will be a blank screen, but what do
we care? Little things like boll weevils keep drilling
at these tender spots until the juice is all gone, pulped
into mandible and larvae, and all the pictures show
that the findings are inconclusive. Things grow
while dying, blossom while falling
apart, stretch in the midst of withering; no beauty

is ever without its rot. The end is merely
roots, clinging to nutrients no longer needed, a whispered
narration as the wind blows the snowflakes. Tomorrow
I'll look for a sapling and call it ancient.

Psalm

> *"Deep calleth unto deep"*
> —Psalm 42:7

These maelstroms, galaxy spirals catching
currents and tying them in knots, boom their
centrifugal voices in defiance of the water
cycle.
        These currents, Chinese dragons
swirling their tails, dipping their heads, chatter
the language of bubble-sprouting trout.
                        These cadmium-throated
drifters, aquatic artillery shells encased
in gravel, leap to serenade
the dragonflies with their gaping
war hymns.
        These dragonflies, goggle-eyed
biplanes, little horses of the devil, chant to
the upturned leaves with their voices
of bassoon.
        These heaven-facing leaves,
coracles of chlorophyll anticipating spinning,
sing their waiting song to the raindrops preparing
to dive from cargo-bellied clouds.
        These speeding
drops of water, sling slung rocks thudding
their impact, plop the chorus of spring into circlets
along the banks, vanishing craters in the currents,
notes absorbed by dynamic-ignoring
waterfalls.
        These right-angle rivers, this pouring
out from pitcher to basin, crescendo their mist
to the cottonmouth clouds.
        These cumulonimbus,
dust bunnies beneath God's bed blown by the breeze
of an opening door, hum a counter melody into the ear of
prismatic sun-bounced air.

                      This air rumbles and shakes
the branches of clouds, pears fall to rot
among the puddles, the puddles flow
across continents and even the maelstroms
know that this chorus repeats.

                      All of creation fermatas.

Perichoresis

An old man dances with oaken buckets
on his feet. It thunders.

Duck-billed egg layers forage for
echidnas. Family reunions are small these days.

Leaves vortex around islands
of grass and sparrows with sprained wings.

Once a month the luna halo shines on
this field of soy bean sprouts

and we dance in the shadow of a moon-shone
oak. We treble and bass the minor shades.

...like doves released at funerals...

They re-buried Yagan's head this week
in soils rich with adiaphora and kingfisher feathers.

I've only seen waves in various stages
of death. In terminal crashing I feel the spray

and know that out at sea, the waters dance
like old men in oaken buckets. It thunders.

On the Eighteenth of January it Rained in Central Ohio Because the Temperature was Forty-Three Degrees Fahrenheit

Where the hill hangs limp like shoes over a power line,
the road's wooded ribcage wheezes its vapors. I drive through
the breath-steam and into the crescendo
of streetlights, front porch lunas, and traffic signals' kelp-forest
glow. Tomorrow promises snow and the road will hold
its breath. I drive through hills that thaw
into puddles, become flat like the unbroken grass
which bows beneath my feet. False rivulets give hope out of the melting
and winter looks different tonight. I know a woman
who is the fourteenth incarnation of Tamarlane.
She delivers newspapers for the Lancaster Eagle-Gazette and sings
karaoke on Wednesday nights at the Orange Carpet.
Jacob stumped and wobbled his way to Israel; change always comes
with a limp. I know a poet who claims to be a truck driver. See how lines blur,
murky like an overcast night? Coming home, the mist is already gone,
pounded into the waiting ground. Earth's axis wobbles
and the clouds limp off to the east.

Circadian

Myth:
where islands Athena out of oceanic godheads;
where coronal rings float on these tides like oil

slicks, reflecting our transience; where biodiversity
clings to bobbing coconut husks; where the blues

meet and blend in shades of parabola and dome—
I'll be clinging to an upturned turtle shell

March:
I don't know.
Maybe I'll eat
the wind and taste
what yesterday was like
to the west. If there's a hint
of juniper, I'll know that the ending
was bad. I'll cry and my tears
will form next month's rain,
puddles for earthworms
to drown in. They turn
into adders and the wind
blows their venom
to the east.

Pax Lunaris:
Hush moon.
I don't care
about your waxing
and waning. We're all in our crescent
stage. You can hope for fullness,
while all we have to look forward to
is the blankness of being
new.

The Last Elegy:
Collapse. All things do.
Stars take eons
to show their shriveled
heads to us. Where we see
twinkling, there could be just a void.
So be careful where you wish—
there may be nothing there.

Speleosis

in bone-floored caves where you can hear the water trickle like
    black keys through canyons of transposed shale

we'll find it

then crawl deeper into caverns lined with afterbirth and etched
    with maps of foreign suns

underground, underwater, underfoliage, underlight,
    undergestation, underdeath

overmagma, over the other side of the world, overgeist, over things
    so deep they'd shatter if they surfaced

you are a we, you are an I; I am someone else

you are omni; I am drawing on the placenta with the ashes of
    ancient sacrifices

the smoke smells of answers and fills this chamber of questions

tomorrow there will be no more bones

Forty Minutes Before Composing an Aubade

The moon is a jaguarundi's eye; it flares
our faces carved into trees—arborglyphs lined with
lichens—our eyes pupiled by bark-winged moths.

Beneath this cuticle crescent, this heat-curled
strip of tree skin, we'll mourn the loss
of permanence and hold each other until the
western
glow gives up its isolation
and smiles its wetwoodsmoke eyes at us.

The moon is impaled on the arm of a quaking
aspen. Tonight this triune water cycle
drops the ridge with sheets of prevenient grace.

Above, the moon rabbit looks down
on our dissonance, our attempts at finding chords
that don't resemble springfrogfields,
the chirpings of water over rocks,
the accidentals of the hind legs of a cricket,
the imagined silence
of five million firefly lanterns and the hum
of five million firefly wings.

When vapor hugs those meteor scars, promising
tears, we'll walk above the tide and bleed
our expectations of rain. Tomorrow night

the moon will hide.

Variations on a Theme by God

My Daughter Changes Her Mind About Shadows

Where heaven pops and spreads like the palm tree heads of frost that grow across
my newly-cleaned windshield in time-lapse, I'm tugged by greater than and feel
reverberations of echolocation. My squeaks and screams bounce
off this map, returning to be devoured by shadows, shadows that once terrified
my daughter. She couldn't find the form within the void; now she waves
to the darkness and knows that sometimes things are better without faces.

I'll caravel this coast, keeping the ridges within my failing waves
of vision, until the shadows create ex nihilo noses and eyes and lips that
recognize me. I told my daughter there was nothing to fear
from shadows—she'd miss them when they were gone. Now I lay in bed, bobbing
through foreign breakers, not recognizing any of the shadows that project upon
        these cenote
walls. Light flickers like the feathers of a quetzal and I glimpse a familiar
        cheekbone.

A Pre-Elegy for Margaret

May 2010

Someday she might die.
She talks at night to moths,
winging bony arms out of her wheelchair
and into the glow of a porchlight.
I suspect that she speaks the dead
language of the Arawaks, words
carried on trade winds from Hispaniola
to Baltimore, Ohio. Her body
a calamus, bent and broken
and chewed by cats, willow strong
and reed thick, one eye hidden
beneath pools of milk and honey,
the other having already seen
that life is what happens between
traumas. She lives life, willing
to wait for the ghosts of family
and roommates to find
her and all of her incomplete parts.
I suspect that when we meet above
the moth-orbited stars,
I will not recognize her.

An Elegy for Margaret

November 2011

An old woman clothed entirely in moths, carefully guarding her
abdomen, hiding her
      exoskeleton, her segmented

secrets. Eyes closed, curtained with fine silk, wrinkled eyelids, their
sad corners descending
      like a river through a canyon. She'll wake

and dry her wings, stretching, her garments full of pupae shells and
the remnants of shape-
      shifting. Cover her with robes of thistle

down, anoint her with petrichor, see her scurry, windblown, embers
stoked, sparks unmoored.
      There is no journey like hers. Catch the falling drops

of wingwet, last remnants of exile, gather the leaves as they float
down laden with words. She is a
      tourniquet of paper,

binding bark with false bark, holding back the flow of four
hundred tomorrows just waiting to fly
      out like bats

from a church with missing bricks. Soon she'll remove her moth-
wing clothes and stride proudly
      up the staircase, one sun

at a time. Soon she'll be so naked I won't recognize her, her wings
crisp with the frost of a
      thousand dark worlds.

The Silence Between Words Can be as Beautiful as all the Gilded Syllables That Stand Out Like Stars Among the Blackgaps of Space

The poet's daughter is three and can't talk.

    He watches her,

        a whole dark city on fire.

Learning to Speak

She found her
      voice while pushing through ferns
and trampling on mushrooms,
         musking the air, spreading spores,
disrupting

                      the hiding places

of deer and consonants. The rocks could
      hear her singing ancient firehymns,
the anthems of a voice in spring.
         With dandelions in her throat,
she warbled

                  seeds

     of next year's hillsides. She's an old nest
     with wet shells and fresh feathers.

On Being Hugged by a Four-Year-Old Stranger

"May I give you a hug?" he asked. "I give really good hugs."
I said sure, and leaned across my stool to his,
his tiny arms reaching around me, his face smothered just below my
armpit. He doesn't let go and I worry
about hugging this child in the front of a restaurant,
waiting for his grandmother to swing
her purse and cudgel
me across the jaw.

        The grandmother passed me
        a napkin-written note, the boy's father
        had died and he's been hugging everyone since.

I wanted to hug him again. I wanted to hug
my daughter. I wanted to hold both of those little
styrofoam cups, so easily crushed, so easily melted.

        He wasn't hugging me,
        he was grasping. I pulled
        away, brushing white flecks
        of him off my shirt, tiny
        moths ashing the shimmering air.

Variation on a Theme by God

When sitting on a bed, sharing
a mattress with a harvested husk,
one must choose to believe in resurrection
or not. There's no maybe while the body
cools and there's no room for uncertainty
when the house is full of last exhalations
and excess air. There's no wrong answer
while mourning sways us, just hints
and lapsed code from the only one in the room
who knows for sure. We listened

sitting at the foot of your deathbed. We made
our own clues. So there, within feet
of your discarded shell clinging
to oak, we announced that we were having a baby.
We'd held it in for four months, waiting
for certainty, setting this as our date
to stop holding our breath. We exhaled
and you did not breathe in.

Thought After Setting Oneself on Fire

Worth

it's amazing how much you miss lips
hers were stream-stone smooth and cool, one kiss
always heated mine

teeth don't burn   I feel them split, porcelain
plates pulled up from the sea   no one appreciates
cracking

these flames make quick heroes but I already feel myself ashing
into the wind, sweeping into the gutters with the cigarettes
and food wrappers   the air tastes of singed
feathers and coffee grounds but I'm forgetting
what lamb tastes like

       perhaps I'm too impulsive

it's gone dark surprisingly fast   the air dances
its penitence, fat and warm from my fuel-offering   I see
sparks from smoldering coals behind my eyes

tomorrow I'll be at sea
tomorrow I'll gather my shards of pottery
tomorrow I'll be a drop of water to the thirsty
tomorrow I'll be a scorch mark on this alley

now is when the scene slows and the music
starts   I'm ready to lie forward
before these firetrucks, surrounded by saffron
speedbumps

don't forget
I gave my lips for this

Sati

I guess death is transferable
I guess death is a woman's role

tomorrow I'll wake and reassemble
my ashes into tusk-ivory

I always thought dying was a
lantern; now I find it's a procession of torches

my arms are finely polished
porcelain and my hair is a tangle of smoke

and melting wax
I despise his flame and the fact that his

is blending in with mine
even in death I can't get a moment

to breathe in the heat of freedom
without his sparks catching my veil

Beneath McNamara's Window

Maybe
tomorrow will break
its skull on the doorframe
of heaven; the sun will forget
everything about today.

These times will surely fill with ocelot
spots. The clouds will migrate
like wild geese. The years will autumn
away until these elemental crystals, painted
like mine-dust, are spored on winds

with no place to land. Forever
is a myth—like peace and love and hope
and trust and pain and forgetting.
Abstractions written in sidewalk chalk
made from bits of ground-up bone.

Tomorrow all will bloom and I will
pollinate. Tomorrow this volcanic town
will wake to a layer of ash. Tomorrow
I will be a sprinkling of spent fuel.
Tomorrow the children will dance
as the shadows creep away toward the east.

Alice Hertz

Eighty-two years is too long
to go without being consumed;
yet they denied me my eschaton,
perfectly planned and executed.
Damn the Samaritans—if only
the president had been driving by.

being the final thoughts of Alfredo Ormando, on fire outside of St. Peter's Basilica protesting the Vatican's condemnation of homosexual Christians

It began with a whoosh, the sound of a mighty rushing
wind, tongues of fire. Who knew that death
whooshed? My sanctification, an instant before
perfection at the feet of God, cauterizes old wounds.

                        It's strange to see my skin sailing
                like so many kites, swirling in these pyric
         winds—the energy released by my disassembling.
              Pontifex Maximus, I hope you smell me
                  singeing in your piazza. My queer flames
carry the scent of anger and pain. They smell like my burned
    brothers, whose ashes mixed with Jews and Gypsies.
                      Now I offer my own embers.

It is not right for the sun to go down
on my anger. I see it sinking beneath the dome,
or perhaps that's my glow rising to meet
the shimmering heavens. Around me swirl dancing
dermal stars, Orion assembling just over my left shoulder.
They're coming now to save me. Everyone's trying
to save me. But wrapped inside this burning
bush I've never felt safer. My chariot idles.

                      I dare you to tell me God
           doesn't love me. He pours out His mercy
        on my billowing. Mercy is rain in the Atacama;
             mercy is when the lion breaks
      the wildebeest's neck; mercy is the blackness
        that envelops my body as it turns to sand.

Wax

I was twenty-two when I started eating candles.
I remember the scent was black raspberry vanilla and it tasted

like the wings of wasps. I bit my cheek
and bled—black raspberry vanilla filled my mouth

so I kept chewing, like a wolf licking a knife
covered in frozen seal blood. That night I dreamed

of cell division, mitosis drenched in plasma and smelling
like candles. Every day I eat a candle, different scents

leading to different flavors, but all tasting like variants
of insecticide. I don't bleed anymore. Now I chew on my cheek

and wax seeps from my mouth like rubber from a tap,
and I chew until my teeth are wax and my tongue is coated

like candy. Tonight I'll wick myself and burn
on this hilltop—a paschal flame to scare away the Sidhe.

Tomorrow gather my ashes into tapers
to place upon the altar, votives to light around the shrine.

Inhale the smoke and taste the lattice-work wings
of a wasp and smell the blood running

from a thousand rivulets carved into wax,
like the shafts dug by a thousand dead miners.

In Remembrance

everywhere evaporation, sweat swept
away before beading

all of the light on this block is mine,
I made it, I shine in the left-turn lane

all around the people watch and set their
compasses, they'll go back to work

tomorrow and write in secret books
what they saw

they'll keep my ashes tucked away
in shirtpockets and the fibers of their eyebrows

one day they'll see a startling of flame
and I will burn again

To Taste the Feet of Bees

An Ant Contemplates the Suddenness of Death

Walking this pheromone
highway, like thousands before me, smelling
yesterday's hope-filled paths, lost
in the history of finding.

        Suddenness

is an aphid revolt—no one can predict

these things. Today

        tomorrow smells like

trails and rubber and looks

like blackness descending. I can feel
my antenna swiveling, seeking,
independent of that part of me that knows
there's nothing left to find.

In Praise of Nomadism

> *"Perhaps an increasingly sedentary lifestyle undermined the Scythians' nomad spirit, leading to cultural collapse."*
> —Mike Edwards in *National Geographic*, September 1996

Sharks cannot stop swimming or they
won't make it to the feeding frenzy in time.
All the choice bites of tuna, the ones
behind the gills and below the dorsal fin,
will be eaten by the transients
who don't have to lock up their shops
and find sitters for their fishlets. Those who stop
to rest or tend their kelp crop are left
with scraps of squid and remoras
that cling to their stomachs.
Remoras taste like oiled reef
and sea turtle shell. Slowly those settled sharks
sink toward sea-bed apathy, never noticing
that they have started to resemble
remoras. The others nomad by,
tugged by a nose-full of seal blood
and migration. In days the seafloor shark
fades into archaeology and tectonics.

And no one misses the giant fish
and the kelp grows taller
and the remoras find a faster ride
and sharks do not excavate tombs.

Rabbit

You should have run away. I clapped
in front of your face, the universal
signal to snap out of hypnosis, I mowed within
inches of clipping your whiskers into a slaw
with the lopped off
clover heads and chastised grass. You twitched,
epileptically still, eyes fixed like Fiver
on the Black Rabbit, seeing everything
but what was there. We scooped you
into a crate, you still stared, shellshocked,
too dull or dazed to even fear. Tomorrow you'll probably

die. The rabbit population will not mourn.
The neighbor kids will be sad
for five minutes. Your mother will never
know, nor wonder. Somewhere a hawk will miss
a meal and a fox will feel the gnaw of hunger
because you turned to glass
wrapped in weeds inside an old milk crate. We'll bury you
among the gravel and think token thoughts
of the fragility of life. But you were flawed, thumbing
your twitching nose at grace.

Bee Stings

   The stinger stands in my forearm like a man wading into the ocean.
     It sentinels, sac strapped to its feet, sunk beneath swelling,
      throbbing the remnants of rage. Soon it will be swept away
        by the unforgiving edge of a MasterCard.

I kicked a fallen wasp today into the corner
of the garage. I watched as it lay still until found by a mobile
village of ants, crumpled, used, wearing its golden
torcs, reclining like the Dying Gaul. Stinger feebly
circling, searching for an end to the torment, watching
as its exoskeleton was disassembled, carried off in trundling
mandibles, each nibble one piece closer to disintegration. I whispered
an apology, turned away, and left the wasp still swinging its stinger,
like the last eagle standard in the Teutoburg Forest.

Maneaters

for the Tsavo maneaters, shot and killed December, 1898

These migratory clouds—unstoppable
wildebeest herds, edges whisping away
like predator-primed stragglers—they watch and shake
their fluffy manes at the jester-thorned barriers
of pruned acacia. Lost among the adiaphora
of railroad construction—the Sanskrit names
of laborers, the burial places of Masai
bones and the remains of lion meat
left to old adversaries—there beat aortic
memories. Look into the glass
eyes of carcasses one hundred years
dead, and gazelle yourself into prey
and the security of dead-branch thorns.

Meditation on the Dried and Severed Back Leg of a Grasshopper

I stared at its serrated side, like the lower jaw
of a thylacine. I felt its frog-leg crook, its density
like a wishbone, anticipating sundering, placing
a wish that will never be spoken or remembered
or hoped for. Today it will find a home
among the other discardae—grass clippings
and the sloughed-off fur of a groundhog. Before it jumped
from my hand, a splinter of wind-caught wicker, I saw

the bleached and hollowed
scapula of a pilot strapped into the cockpit
hundreds of feet below the point where the horizon
dips itself into the baptismal waters of the Pacific.

      And then it's gone.

Somewhere out there a five-legged grasshopper
has not been taught to mourn. I would mourn
for it, but all of my sadness is locked
up in glaciers, waiting to crack and calve
when the world warms and tears thaw from their bondage.
So I'll let the wind blow it off of my finger,
like an eyelash after making a wish. Standing in my garage

I'll wish for wholeness, for the return
of leaping and all things
displaced. I could look for it among
the chaff, but some things are best left
unrecovered. Sometimes completeness is a myth
worth constructing. I walk inside and the building
continues.

Dead Sunflowers

bowing, their beehive
faces hidden, penitent
as if the earth could offer
some relief from the tilt
of its own axis—fallen
monoliths unattended
and gravitied, decaying
redwoods toppling
to ancestor-holding
loam, failed insurgents
hanging upon this crucifix
of autumn, pleading
resurrection—they'll never
taste the feet of bees again

Until Our Arms are Masts and Our Songs are Sails

Thresholds

> *"I am standing today on the threshold of another trembling world.
> May God have mercy on my soul."*
> —Bobby Sands

Today I'll try and tremble the timbre
of God's mercy. Today I stand, not through the door, but in
its whalemouth jaws. Behind me, the table is full

of water; bills and last night's dishes float across its surface
on shoals tugged by the overhead lamp. Abalone shell
to the east, the sky a soap dish, through the doorway

I can glimpse disappearing
stars, their glass-water clarity fading to pale
forgetfulness. Where do they go?

What did Bobby think about, there in Long Kesh,
as the world began to quiver like the legs
of a satisfied lover? He could see his ribs

glowing on the dermal walls of caves,
about to be erased by the rising
waters of an underground river, but could he smell

the water? Behind me the water rises, spilling
over the table, carrying documents over its falls and onto
the floor. I walk through the door and lay down

on this bed, this whale fluke floating among
kelp and discarded pajamas. Alone,
I lay my head in the shallows and sleep.

Inter-Oceanic Love Song

Atlantic:
I miss you like Cameroon
misses Brazil. Things once joined
feel naked after continental drift.

Pacific:
*At night, as I sway, I dream of your squalls,
your doldrums, the thickness
of your Sargasso. Tomorrow I'll rejoin
your today. My life crawls over mountains,
flows uphill through lochs, breaks through this isthmus
that so foolishly divides. Erosion always wins.*

I want you to engulf me, swallow me in your
eddies and gyres. Become so full of me that you spill
over coasts until I ring your fire without fear
of evaporation.

*I want to tierra our fuego
and feel the place where our waters
meet. We blend so beautifully that ships
capsize in the boil of our straits.*

I'll never forget the nights we spent circling
Pangaea. I dream of them when I'm lying beneath
clattering hulls and the bobbing bellies
of seabirds. When the tide hits just right
I can still taste your salt, the memories
of reefs we once shared.

*One day, my love, we'll spill over
Patagonia and exchange whaleribs and lingerings
of ichthyosaur. I'm boiling for you, melting
my extremities, not stopping until I lap
your shores and warm your cold currents.*

Promise me you'll find me soon. My shorelines
tingle with your vibrations.

Love makes no promises
when tides are involved. But I will keep
churning, clawing at the boundaries, trickling
through cracks in the soil and evaporating
into rain to fall on you. Look for my puffins
and know that I'm thinking of you.

I'll send you something soon, caravel sails
and waterlogged charts, bones of fellow
migrants and indigenous species of crustaceans.
Pry off my remoras and barnacles from passing
keels and taste southerly brine. I'll pass the sun
to you tonight, tattooed
with a message of longing.

I put the sun to rest and wait for the day
it hovers over our waters like Yahweh
on the day we first met. My trenches are still
full of you. Tomorrow is one drop closer
to immersion.

I've sunk islands waiting for you.

Is that regret I hear in your breakers?

I'll gladly sink more, until islands are only
a memory to haunt leviathan, a home to groupers,
city streets to be walked by krill and swept
by carpet sharks.

I love your westward currents.

I love your rafts of thatch and koala hair.

Let's exchange lava, bubble together and hiss
our defiance to embryonic land.

Until you swallow the sun, I'll wait for you.

When I swallow the sun, I want you
to feel the warmth.

Amelia

Alone, she moved campfires
out of forgetfulness and a sense of wandering natural
to one with nothing to do but watch constellations

in trans-oceanic flight. She must have wondered
how it would end. Or perhaps her bearings were past
the point of horizon identification. She was a turtleshell,
upturned, longing for fullness, wishing she could coracle

to the base of the sun. She plotted her next course,
took sextant readings on cloudy midnights, knobbed
the short-wave under surf-spray, waiting for
clearance from the tower. She sang Lady of Spain

until the crabs scattered her wreckage like
Tiamat across this coral-starred lagoon.

Atoll

for Mal

Somewhere Amelia is composting
coral and composing hermit crab homes
with her delicate calcium, tiding
to one side like a halibut's migrating
eye. I see you gathering samples
of sand seeded with bits of log
book and emu feathers. Where waves
irregularly nibble at your toes, where you
can irregularly beat back
their advances. Perfect timing

doesn't occur in nature—even migratory
pods of cetaceans sometimes drift
into San Francisco Bay—perhaps eternity
is rhythmic, but scholars have debated
that for centuries. Amelia knows—
instruments can only get you so far;
the rest is up to the winds and the tug
of the moon. But your sandbar is far
from desolate. There are lots of ratites
and fellow wrecks. So we'll dance

around the fire tonight in the glorious
random of flame-flight, praising
the fact that the reef is alive.

A Glossary of Nautical Terms

anchorage
> *To hold the breath of oil*
> *and kelp. The crab-crawled*
> *bed is fertile and waiting for*
> *the sinking of metal.*

belay
> *The strings that hold*
> *our vapor suspended on tides*
> *of carbon dioxide. Snip*
> *them and watch the rain*
> *fall, dropping exhalations.*

doldrums
> *Stop looking at me, Afghan Girl.*
> *I don't want to look at your*
> *refugee eyes. These masts blaze*
> *with the fire of electric*
> *saints and I can't look away.*

gybe
> *The fickleness of chin*
> *ook winds, the type*
> *writer dart of shoaling blue*
> *fin, the zig and zag of an end*
> *less journey.*

luff
> *The part of your words that slice*
> *the air like a marlin back, until*
> *I can't catch my shorn breath.*

rogue wave
> *//We all know that gypsies*
> *are unpredictable//We never expect*
> *despots to happen here//The juntas*
> *have no power on this river//Chart*
> *the waves, but check the sextant,*
> *the stars play tricks on the waters//*

wake vs. wash
>*Saigon rooftops in 1975 vs. the Central Highlands in 1969*
>*cenotes vs. inter-island tides in the Faroes*
>*post-butterflied cocoons vs. the roll of caterpillar fuzz*
>*you are gone vs. you are here*

yaw
>*The horizon-peeking sun, the chameleon*
>*moon, blue & white & scarred. Dirvishing*
>*waters, spinning so fast the fore and aft*
>*keep popping over the glass*
>*at the end of the ocean. Tomorrow*
>*we'll stop the carousel and love*
>*the eternity of today. There, on plastic*
>*wrap waters we'll meet the drifting*
>*hulls of ancient caravels and share*
>*secrets of navigation. We'll row*
>*until our arms are masts*
>*and our songs are sails.*

St. Brendan Sails to the Moon

Slipping free from the moorings
at the edge of the Dingle Peninsula, curragh
tanned & trimmed & cargoed with freeze-dried
salmon and herring, towed to sea by a tug
of seals, the mariner waits for the wind.

To sail by stars takes new meaning when the cords
of *terra firma* are snipped between the teeth
of a whale, and off we fly into the trumpet-blast
darkness. Stars seem even farther out here,
refraction makes all things seem closer.

Passed by remnants of orbitals, eternal
flotsam, tiding through the obsidian shoals.
Our rising hymn, our vespers prayer, all chanted
beneath the curved edge of space, the distance
of light to light. Somewhere out here

we'll find it. We rise like our songs, like corks,
like Fionn at the call of the bugle. Everywhere
we're surrounded by nowhere. Tomorrow
has no meaning, no rotation, no sun to set our
prayers by; so we sail these fierce currents

and toss the charts to the stars shaped like
marlin spikes and close our eyes to block out
the darkness. We arrive on the rocks of Tir na nOg
and find that the Land of the Blessed holds
no air. Wrapped in this nebula

of solitude, twice finding that which was never there,
we set our backs to the oars and turn
once again toward Ireland. We'll re-enter
and burst into flames. When we next see the dawn
it will be as mariners of vapor, sailing toward

heaven on petrel wings, spinning like a coracle
among the breakers. The moon will watch
and pull us toward the promised land and clouds
will be our whaleback beaches, carrying us closer
to the one who wrote our sailing songs and poured our seas.

We'll not look back until our ring cross sail
dips beneath the waves and God closes His eyes
to black out the darkness.

Parts Left Over After Translating Dichotomy

You think you're looking at a coastline; you're pretty
sure it's a lake. See the lighthouse beams, swaying in the clouds
like low-lying fruit? You could pluck them and the lighthouse
would never know—it's historic and unmanned and the light's
as real as courage. You blink and everything stays the same,
which is not what you expected. You blink again.

This rock, this one directing the inlet tide, this one that looks
with submerged eyes browed in kelp, you've seen it before. It's been
      watching
you, memorizing your movements until it knows when you're going to
      breathe
like it knows when the next wave is coming. You look past it,
pretend you didn't notice, a girl at a school dance ignoring
the fat kid in the corner. You seal your eyes with melted lighthouse
      beams

and open them days later. The rock is gone, slunk home to leak
its salt among the barnacles. You hear the gulls chant the Torah,

Esau was a hairy man;
Jacob was a smooth man.

You know that to bleed right now would take too much effort.

The waves get shorter, unable to reach
the coast, the space between a wriggling mass of jellyfish
stings and seasnake bites. It will rain soon

and the light will be extinguished and the rock will sing
with the gulls and you'll blink and dance with your arms half-way
      around
the fat kid and he'll whisper something you'll never hear and tomorrow
will be full of blinking and losing and misappropriation

of lighthouse beams. The gulls will be talking about you with the
        suddenness
of the first rain drop. How you're hairy and smooth and covering
        your arms
with kelp and scraping your legs with rock shavings and you'll blink
like you've never blinked before, a strobe of blinking, until
        everything moves
in slow motion, frame-by-frame-by-frame-by-frame and you watch
        Hektor
and Akilles sparring in hell, each knowing what the other's going to
        do, but unable
to care. You blink and while your eyes are closed you see Esau shaving.

Cell Phone Pictures of the Inside of My Pocket

Similes Written for Accompaniment on the Hurdy Gurdy

Because its wheel spins like an extra-solar planet, waggling
in the darkness of space like a bee with the taste of honey
still stuck to its legs like asteroids sucked in by the gravitational pull
of shin hair.

Because it looks like some sort of flounder, lying on its side,
eyes in migration, singing its mermaid song and playing its scales
like a humpback warming up, tuning to the key of deep water like
an alto dugong.

Because its strings hum the same note, like the air outside
of Taos, New Mexico, constant, immutable, like God's
haircut, which everyone knows is shoulder-length and sedimentary
like the rocks outside of Lancaster, parted by highway.

Because its strings are made of gut, intestinal vibration like
the holy bowels of saints, emptied on the side of a pilgrimage
road, like piles of remembrance stones on the unpromised side
of the Jordan.

Because it plays with fingers pushing wedges, lined up from neck
to hand, reaching away like center-line reflectors on a highway
that stretch and arc like a sauropod's neck, wearing a patchwork
of shadows like a topographical map of the Gaeltacht.

Because its bridge buzzes like the timer on a dryer with its load
of clothes spinning like Sufi mystics, like water glubbing toward
a drain, like extra-solar planets, like the wheel
of a hurdy gurdy.

Red

All the beetles are dying, sucked up
in vacuum cleaners, ground
into red dye, trapped in winterized
window sills. No one mourns
them—they're just beetles. These
days I cling to cluttered panes, grabbing
glass against the pull of cleaning
suction. My red is not for sale. Red is sacred

to the Sentinelese islanders.
It doesn't have to be good
red, it could be a slip of construction
paper, the kind my daughter scissors
into snowflakes. They dive on anything
hinting at red. They're barbarians
though and everyone knows

barbarians love red. If you crushed
the Sentinelese, they'd give off red
powder. No one would mourn
them—no one's even talked to one;
we know more about beetles. If the beetles
and Sentinelese were both cycloned
to a remote part of Patagonia
we would notice the lack

of beetles. I wish I spoke the language
of red. That would keep me from being ground
into cake. I'd return all the gifts
of ribbon and watercolor and leave
Patagonia of my own volition.
God cries tears tinged with scales

from a cutthroat trout—cadmium
and shimmering
with exoskeleton. The Sentinelese
scramble to collect the tears
and align them in holy constellations
on their window sills. We'll never miss
the stars when they fall.

Cell Phone Pictures of the Inside of My Pocket

—the void between stars,
    the valleys of the moon,
 the distant forests nighted
    into the horizon—

        —my anthracite heart—

    —close-up of brow fur
        on a ferret—

—what Lazarus saw
    before light invaded
        sarcophagal eyes
          and blinded visions
of paradise—

        —the wing of a starling, minus
          its purple sheen—

    —oil, oh
    so much oil—

—my daughter's pupil,
    reflecting my fear—

        —the place where
        monsters [hide]—

        —a total lack of focus—

—hope when the entire frame
    tells me not to—

An Instruction Manual for Flight

Begin by flapping your arms. Hold
your breath; oxygen disbursement is crucial.
We've included extra parts. The pancreas
is entirely useless for flight. If you have vestigial
webbed toes, we encourage you to use
them; we will not supply
extra skin. While flapping your arms,
release air slowly and hum a C sharp. If your packaging
did not include a C sharp, please purchase
a companion kit (*see appendix F*); if you cannot
sing, then you will simply have to walk; operating this product
a cappella can lead to serious injury and even death.
And it voids your warranty (*see appendix J*). Remember
to register your product with the FAA and understand
all legal aspects (*see appendix R*) pertaining
to federal no-fly lists. None of this is applicable
if you live in a state containing
the letter O. In those cases, the flapping
should take place *after* the release of air and the note
should be a C natural. By purchasing this product you waive
all rights to legal action should you be sucked
into turbines, hit by migrating geese, or strike
a mountain hidden by a nebula of cloud cover.
While still flapping your arms and humming,
measure the wind velocity to the closest knot and site
in on the nearest buoy. For non-coastal flyers,
you'll still need to find a buoy (*for tips on inland buoy spotting,
see appendix BB*). It will be helpful at this point to learn
Arawak, proto-Aztecan, and Ogham, as the rest of the instructions
are in Old Church Slavonic. Thank you for purchasing this product,
and we wish you happy flying. Remember,
it's not flying unless you're off the ground
(*In some states, this may not be true, or may be more
stringent. Michigan, for example, mandates flight
as beginning at 1 foot, seven inches. For more information
see appendix GW*).

Addendum: Due to recent court action, we are obligated to tell you that there is no medically proven method of human flight; we simply misread a drawing by Leonardo Da Vinci. We appreciate your understanding and please do remember that all sales are final and non-refundable. Thank you and keep sending us those in-flight pictures!

D.B. Cooper Dreams of Falling and Wakes to the Taste of River Stone Behind His Uvula

Every time, I wake somewhere
above the trees. It's dark, but I can smell them
below, rippling with rainwinds, their mouths
moving but making no sound. I know they're talking
about me. Once, I heard them singing potlatch
songs so I gave them rafts of greed and they made me
their chief. In that particular tomorrow
I wrapped myself in a tarp of flattened
raindrops and danced with wings strapped to my branches,
their tips the color of stormsetting sun. Peace is floating
near the bank among the rusty needles. I saw it
once, beneath the salmon tongue
of a deer, riding the ripples and disappearing
downstream. Perhaps I'll find it in the next
tomorrow. Nights are bad. It's worse when it rains.
My hip's been drained
of marrow and filled with the currents
of every navigable river west of the Continental Divide.
I forget how it ends. I think I beheld Satan
fall like lightning from heaven.

D.B. Gives Instructions on Falling

Before abandoning everything, you must make sure you grab
the extra parachutes. Don't look up or down,
only out, straight ahead, and eventually you will slip on the leaves
like an ephod, thrust into them, your phallic
fall enough to free you from your strings. Bend your knees or watch your hips erupt
the shock and awful tingle of sudden cessation. If all things fall, distinguish
yourself by falling fastest—terminal velocity be damned. I'm telling you,
landing is the easiest part.

we all fall down, ringing around
these scaffolds and pyres

Who holds your freedom? Your descent is a time to ponder
how flies get inside the windows, between the glass
and the screen, when to take off your coat in the car—that moment
of apricity in mid-February, how two hundred thousand dollars can be so
heavy. Wear denim and skydance your pain
to the raindrops. Hold out your hands and try to clutch
the rope thrown to you
by God. You'll miss.

we all fall down, riding around
these ashtowers and cylinders of slag

Don't let the yarn run out; you'll need it to find
your way back to the sky. Sip the toxins beneath this tarpaulin
and tell your fellow fallers that tomorrow
would have been a better day
to jump.

we all fall down, rimming around
these ravines holding remains of rumor

Upon Exiting the Highway and Entering a Town in Southern Ohio

The lights all crowd around the exit, like claustrophobes
getting out of an elevator. The air here is used. All around, everyone
hunches. Hunching shows their love of feet. Their feet smoke
with a thousand cigarettes internalized through the left kidney
and out the fourth toe. Retired mine canaries are rehabbed for work
as instant messengers while retired miners are rehabbed for work
as garden gnomes, their noses already red and internal organs
already made of plaster. Everywhere the townspeople are seeking
modulation, hoping that the next key will be the right one—they crescendo
anyway. The lights here are funny, plum where they should be green,
teal where they should be red, no yellow to speak of.
The exit is across from the entrance. You could keep going
and never notice that everyone is hunched.

Tonight they'll all fly. Everyone will uncrinkle their wings and swirl
like light-drunk moths, weaving in and out of the hemlock,
watching the cars on the highway who never stop, never slow,
never look to the side of the road unless something dead lies there.
The sign, glowing spring and reflecting transience, is just another
name, another mileage, another place to stop and get gas or pee,
but not a place to stay or to dare allow your words to leave
the safety of your mouth. The music stops, an empty mine,
the last chord is left unresolved. Get back on the highway.
There's nothing to see here.

Arpeggios of Defiance

Address to the Nation

For the record, I am completely against genocide.

My administration has always been anti-ethnic
cleansing. When I saw people banded like
numbat tails, I spoke out. When I saw the wobble
of earth's axis, I gave a speech on the injustice of it all.
When the shelling began, I hunkered in abandoned
mine shafts with the moles and the salt and wiped
the tears from babies' eyes with canary feathers. My credentials
are as pure as the fibers on the Shroud of Turin and just as tainted
with the mitochondria of deity. These accusations

will not deter us. Our mission remains the same: to unite
all particles into one great gamma burst of self-actualization
until the bang of all things pops like a cork gun. Come,
let us unwrap the world together, let us dust the spindles
of this balcony with echidna spines, let us gape

when the world breaks apart into shades of mollusk shell
and narwhal tusk. In those days we will sing
until our mouths are full
of blood. Then we'll crescendo arpeggios of defiance
until the refugees see that the world is cracking
and it is safe to come home.

In Anticipation of the Anniversary of a Death

"I'm burning! I'm burning!"
—*Neda Agha-Soltan*

wood-smoke morning, raven cry
scratching the half light

•

I see eyes
in the acorn fingertips
of oaks; the spent shells of locusts
cling to trunks and remember
the feeling of fullness

•

one year later
constellations have migrated
one click of the telescope, stars that died
before the Flood are showing their
faces of death to Earth—we're late
in mourning their passing

•

the wood-smoke lingers
and my feet are wet
with the tears of the grass

Prayer at the Birth of a Nation

July 8, 2011

Tonight I listen to the thunder shake
the rain from the clouds, like drops of dew
when I bump the branches of the apple tree
outside my back door.

In Juba, where bombs once fell
like apple-drops, where streets once trembled
like branches of thunder, people danced
and sang. The Western journalists

and experts called it a "pre-failed" state.
Lord, I'm glad your love extends
to the pre- and post-failed. Tonight I celebrate
a nation in various states of failure

while listening to those beads of water
that were too weak to hold on. May we all
learn to be shaken.

To an Artist with Broken Hands

for Ali Ferzat

lamp lighter, shadow caster, dancing
figure on the cave wall creator, illuminate

every lanyard
of muscle, every split-end of bone, every cord
that holds you together swirls and sketches
new glories, new calls to prayer,
like minarets
swollen with blood

lamp lighter, give me your crippled
matches and I will strike them with trembling fingers

Elegy on a McDonald's Sign

On the sign that sits
below the obnoxious yellow M,
there reads a memorial to a nineteen-year-old
girl, a manager there, killed in a car crash:

> *We love you Kayla, and we'll remember you always.*

I pulled around the drive-through, thinking
of mortality instead of cheeseburgers, and looked
up while ordering to the westbound side
of the sign:

> *Two McChicken Sandwiches and Two Large Fries*
> *$4.99*

Upon Hearing of the Death of Osama Bin Laden

I'm told that to be American is to hate
him; that to be American is to celebrate his death.
Perhaps I'm not
American enough. I hate. I hate the trees
when they disrobe in December and point
their crooked digits at my downcast
scapulas. I hate my
nose and its tendency to take on the shape
of a harpoon when I smile. I hate arrogance
in defeat, bared fangs sneering on a raccoon
splattered across the eastbound lane. Tomorrow

we'll wake to a world minus one murderer.
To be American is to cheer. They're cheering now
outside the White House like we just won
the World Cup. Tonight we invoke God
while David slinks away from Saul's bathroom-cave
with a handful of robe and a face full of shame.

You have heard it said, 'Love your neighbor and hate
your enemy.' But we have since been told to love and pray
for our enemies. Tonight we revert and revel
and rejoice that Hell holds no Americans.

Pick up your stones, brothers. He was worse than us.
Pick up your stones, sisters. The dogs will lick his blood.
Pick up your stones, America. God must be asleep.
We are the vengeance we seek.

The Gentler Tortures

on Guy Fawkes Day

When children die—a firing
squad. When children are abducted—the sudden
straightness of rope. When children ask
where mommy went—a torture, pulling

nails from nails, the relentless tug
of equal and opposite motions.
When children live with leaking
noses, when they carry their skin in

their pockets, when they eat flakes
of dandruff and wash it down with the vapor
of low-lying clouds the color of well-chewed
gum—a gentler torture,

the castaway alone, mouth open, collecting drops of rain, believing
that with enough ocean, the tongue will become a raft.

Of Love and Limerance

Love Poem

Understanding love is like trying to shove
a cat through a juicer. My heart crackles

like shrimp shells and water pouring over ice.
Your voice sounds like a fawn's first steps

and the breathing of trees. Reach
up my pants to the engorged

leech lancing out of my thigh. It's full
of me and my fullness of you. Pull it out

and stop the bleeding. You parasite.
I love our symbiosis. You wear on me

like years of socks that have left my shins
shiny and smooth, vestiges of the glacial properties

of elastic cotton—my hair will never grow
the same. Deciding about you is like

eating live octopus, a linguini of legs
each seeking the nearest path

to salvation. One day I might figure it out
and celebrate by drinking a cat.

Uttering the Holy

Tonight let's utter. Let's murmur. Let's mumble
like troughing sows. Let's whisper sacred

tonight until our breath-steam sparkles with raindrop
spider threads and smells of incense. If everything is said right,

tonight will be our resurrection. We'll see a limping,
a wobble, an unsteadiness, and know that

tonight the trees are blazed with the claws of a ground
sloth and the sparks from escaping heat.

Tonight the fugitive gods are close. They smell like
an earthworm's mating call, like the droppings of stars

tonight releasing their ambergris onto shimmering
sardines, assembled in the keel. Those gods are watching

tonight, hiding from the dogs, using the knowledge gathered
from cowboy movies. When the quiet blasts

tonight, kiss me with your lips stained
with piñon. I'll forever carry

tonight's flavors, the way your hair tasted,
the aroma of your pelt, the way you lifted your face

to the night and dared deities to show themselves
or we would go on disbelieving. Surrounded by discord

tonight, we inhale exhalations, wetting our lungs
with someone else's saliva, regurgitating

the night until our utterings are pure as holy
slivers from the True Cross. We'll pierce our love
tonight and drink the tonic that flows, satisfying
whispered desires and vacant-eyed idols.

Tonight clues will hang from branches like
Houdini over a gorge and the gods will moth

to our night-songs on crinkled wings still wet
from our vapor.

We're Kings Among Runaways

You smell like salt. I don't like you

taking chances with stray cats—I've lost track
of our immunizations. These back alley
pine groves, lit by a lunar
amulet swinging slowly from the neck
of a slender sky, welcome us
bitterly. They know we don't belong, you smelling
like salt, me barnacling to you, both of us whispering
language laden with diphthongs. Seriously,

get a hold of yourself, you smell like
Lot's wife. Beneath a seasoned sky we'll howl
at the cats and start a thousand fires
to mock the stars. We're totems,

you and I, talisman and taliswoman,
hanging beneath conifer chins. They'll come looking

for us and find only an echo, a hint
of the sea, and a vague sense of swinging.

Post Coitum Omne Animal Triste Est

Once our commerce is over, let us go on
        sharing, private and alone in our downcasting,
            swallowing all the pills that bitter
the lining of our oracles like coffee grounds, until
        we peel internally, esophagus shavings trickling
        down our throats. Stay beside me as I lay here
leaving, drifting through these sheets, searching for
        the moment before God rested. We sleep crowded
           but alone, never dreaming
                the same dream—never knowing
                    what each other has forgotten. But such is the way
                      things are supposed to be.

On Dreaming of the Future

Of course, the sun returns. I hear its
glissando creeping
up the bars
of cloud and contrails. I roll
toward the rising and your eyes reflecting
Neptune, lost in your atmosphere,
your revolving, your angry storm—anchored
but beautiful. Even in my daydreams

you are fierce and uncontrollable,
a river wild, straining against the dam, seeking
banks who forget your currents
until
it rains. Staring into
my lagoon-reflection, I need
to see myself in your waters. Without you
I'll shrivel and dry

like a salted slug. In the morning, staring
over your shoulder toward the sun-haired
ridges, I love you
and feel my gulches fill
with your echoes, the cells of a winter
wasp nest reused with the arrival of spring. Our love
is wrapped
in the green that coronas

the blue in your eyes. When they sing
of cedar and piñon, I'll harmonize your conifer
song of longing and cling
to you as the ceiling
begins to rain. We'll lay beneath this pine needle
blanket until we float
to the cleft between the ridges where
the sun rests every morning. I kiss

your shoulder and taste the salt
of ancient seas. I choose not to
gaze, hating its passivity; instead I look
at you like a batter seeking a gap
in the infield. The sun has left
the window
and you have left
the airport.

Adiaphora

the way your hair smells
like ripened barley

your hands that hold as permanently
as graves, as softly as a cat's teeth
on the neck of a kitten, warm and pulsing
like the veins of a volcano

the insignificance of your smile
it mutes when your eyes
sing of the upper left corner and the rising
of steam on soaked pavement, lingering
breath of fallen leaves

when you sprout
new-growth bramble thickets, you mistakenly think
that I care   I don't   I'd climb
through nettle nests to get to you, touch you
if you were covered in barbs of electric eels, caress
your shins if they were serrated
like the porpoise-mouthed legs of a grasshopper

when you sweat you smell
like dandelions and young
stalks of wheat

if we made love
for the last time, I'd not miss it
if I could watch
you dress each morning, undress
each night, touch you
by accident in the hallway

you make nothing matter

Lines in Praise of Pacing

> *"Don't try to rush things:*
> *for the cup to run over,*
> *it must first be filled."*
> —Antonio Machado

I.

Your lips are not conducive to taking
it slow. Your rain-on-pond-water voice
sounds of quickening and poor judgment.
Tonight I've reached terminal velocity
with nothing to slow me
but the ground.

II.

The ground retains the remnants
of last night's rain—it's rained for six days
and the ground is overflowing.

The grass tastes the patience of clouds
and earthworms move across the wet pavement
like mambas. Tomorrow's evaporation

will find them scattered and dried driftwood
across the floor of my garage. Below the grass
the world is still wet.

III.

Slowly starts the morning, until the sun spills
over the ridges. A dust-filled spotlight
comes through the curtains and your face
is a still-life, a portrait, a study in honoring
the moment. I wake you.

IV.

My cup
is full
but filled
with antifreeze

In my haste
I thought
it was
Kool-Aid

Forgive me
for thinking
it was
real

V.

I'd rather die quickly than linger
I'd rather pour quickly than measure
I'd rather be plucked than molt
I'd rather be raptured than pleasured

VI.

Peace comes dropping slow, but war
plummets like teenage hearts.

I am at war this morning,
too impatient for peace.

It doesn't matter. One always fades
into the other, like day into night

and night into day and love into fear
and fear into realizing that you are alone.

VII.

Today I remembered your lips
and the sound of your voice
on the surface of the waters.

I poured myself a drink
and let it run over the lip
like water over a levee.

By the end of the morning
I was sitting on the roof waiting
for the angry wings of a helicopter.

It didn't rush and I drowned.

Beneath the Burning

Vision Quests Terminate in Passages from the Farmer's Almanac

Green smells like morning, night gives
off the scent of black
cherries and covert
hills. My nose is full
of scurrying and I exhale
monotheism. I'm bleeding
from the barbed-wire
back of a bluegill. The tribes
will use those spines for spears
and tip them with nightshade.
I see the howl

of justice, the insomnia
of peace, the antiquity
of war. It all tastes like the shards
of broken wings. I'm stepping

on toads. They squish
with heresy. I wipe my feet
on the lunar halo. Tomorrow
it will rain. I see the brown fur
on a pupating butterfly.
It will be a long winter.

I wake to the smell of green
cherries, the flavor of brokenness
still smeared on the window.

Kairos Hymn Fragments

freshly cut grass, departed
rain, parousial fragrance, asphalt stained
with chlorophyll and cloudfall,
I stand on the porch watching
as clouds and cars bedouin east
to the unrained hills

I can hear the voice
of deity speaking
some extinct language—
an aboriginal tongue long lost
to modern machinery and hybrid
corn

the fullness of time
the Kingdom of God is at hand

watching a rib-furred deer
limp the backyard at one
in the afternoon

Yahweh speaks in the Morse code
clicks of Khoisan bushmen
the feeling of thinking
I forgot to turn off a light
before leaving on vacation

bark-clinging locust shells,
resurrectory hollowness,
oil-drowned sea turtles
covered in eternity

of course, this is all orologically speaking
the end of the day look west
the oriole-feathered sky glowing

luminescence of Eschaton
standing in the trilobite driveway straddling
the International Date Line where one foot's
tomorrow is the other's today

whisper a psalm in God's dead
language, and fill my head with
scents of departure.

Travelogue

to the northeast, Pittsburgh burns
the sky, glows like a radioactive
peach, blends the edges of darkness

●

three hundred and thirty miles across the state of Pennsylvania,
mountains wearing fog-coats, covering their bodies blossoming
with fox fur

●

tonight I dined alone, the only
person in this Italian restaurant on the banks
of the Delaware, from there I went to my reading
which no one attended

●

six more hours alone, listening to poetry
in my car, an audience of
tendons and weary eyes, resisting
sleep and longing for rusty
Pittsburgh.

●

I read in Pittsburgh, full house,
twenty people and three cats, shelves full and hugging
the walls like the inscribed sides of an ancient
tomb, the reading punctuated
by the fists of a listener, silencing
teenage hecklers outside

●

I pull into my driveway, Saturday sun
sparkling the wet grass, to my alone-den house,
breaking the seal of solitude with
the creaking of a door

●

oh, if only every solitude
was as beautiful as mine,
if only every moment alone
was this very moment when
I am all the company I need

●

that night I hugged
my daughter, felt her glow radiate
through my body, and was thankful
for the fog and the leaves that enveloped
the mountain

After Certain Latin American Poets

After our words have all been used, crushed
cans and mosquito-nest tires in the lexiconal
landfill, we'll begin to speak in scents. Aromas
will become our verbs and we'll pungent our
mourning, singe nosehairs with our anger, scent
the cancer that eats at our vital organs like rats
at the feet of Appalachian babies. When we forget

how to smell we'll turn to speaking in urges and finally
bathe in waves of moon-pulled waters that lap and lick
at our coastlines until all of our lives erode
into cliff-beached islands, home to anchorites,
gulls, and bones of giant auks. Then we'll turn
to communicating in excavations, layers
of death and seismic activity, where time is marked

by catastrophes. When we've exhausted all of our
epochs, we'll speak in underwater silence, lips
moving, bubbles climbing toward heaven, relieved
that we're no longer bound to the ropes that suspend
from our teeth and our tongues and carry on
infinitely like the waves of sound sent into space
searching for someone to listen.

Beneath the Orca Sky

Tonight the underbelly clouds tint
the northeast with a nocturnal
nimbus. This is how the eschaton
will arrive—like one a.m.—dawn,
a cloudburst nova, phosphorus
flares over the Ia Drang, a forest
offered to gods of fire. We'll stare
out the patio window, mothing the glow
until the glass shatters and we are free
and small against the light-cracked sky.

I watch the lighted vapor, feel
the cloud-wet grass and know
that tonight, beneath the burning,
are hundreds of parking lot angels.

Streetcorner Parousia

                      Tonight I'll prophesy of moths and brilliant
                shades of wren. Tomorrow I'll scorch the earth
           and retreat to the east of the rubble-city. Tonight
              I'll light the paschal fires on the hills outside
                    the capital. Tomorrow I'll catch cupfulls
              of rain and pronounce them the tears of God.

           Night and day and all the in-between parts
    rub at my cancerousness and break open my scarab shell
        scabs. Look at me, tide-locked, an orbiting mass
    of polarity, and tell me I'm not beginning to resemble
              a gibbon. Over the savannah breaks

the glass of asteroidal dust and skeletal fragments of dead
and broken mountains. If I sweep it up, can I assemble
a diaspora? Maybe tomorrow I'll dress in feathers
of a killdeer and shrill my cry to the cloud-flocked sky
and no one will ever know
that the world is ending.

Another Rainy Day Poem

Stand above a puddle. Make sure you're on the windward side.
Stare into the water nearest the western shore and count
the fleets. Look at their sails tinged with
narwhal tusk, their hulls dipped in

petrichor, their banks of oars protruding like
water-bug legs. On the eastern coast see
the city. Squint at its port, its stag beetle
towers, its revetment against the tide,

its beautiful impermanence. There are millions
of these settlements, star-numbers of these fleets,
all spawning like mosquitoes in the detritus
of precipitation. Look closely because they'll be gone

tomorrow—raptured into clouds, sucked into asphalt
hell-crags, or simply trickling off to new oases
in someone else's driveway. Blooming in the eschaton
of falling water, knowing that the next cumulonimbus

is only a portage away, they'll navigate these pocks
and pot-holes. As real as children and as false
as childhood, leave them to their voyaging;
tomorrow calls for evaporation.

Echolocations of Prayer

The Glory of God is Man Fully Alive

My fingernails are womanishly
long; I always forget to cut them.
This isn't living. All of the upkeep,
empty dawns after clouded
out stars, all of this longing
for the sea has made me
hydrophobic. So I set up
my thalasocracy in exile, trying
to catch the scent of salt
crowded out by falling freshwater.

Miles inland and always dry, touched
by God and limping, longing
to melt this anchor into idol
broth, I'll watch for the exact moment
that night becomes morning.
When the sun arrives, the moon
goes see-through and I can see
that it is nothing but a snowflake
cut with safety scissors
and the belief that all things come out
right when unfolded. I'm awake,

my nails are cut and I can see
through the celestial bodies.
The coast will find me soon and all
will be well. No angel songs
yet—but I thought I heard
humming from somewhere
behind the moon.

For Ramadan: Dawn and Sunset

I look out my back door, seeing hills

                      War plovers this coastline, plundering

and ridges in various shades

                      sea turtle eggs. Tonight I understand

of distance. The farthest so blue-grey

                      the warlord hunger of waves. The erosive
                      qualities

they blend with this morning sky into tones

                      of the moon are ironic for a satellite

of Ursprache. They condense into one

                      still stained with scars and ocean floor

slate-leafed ridge, shorn of its bumps

                      footprints. Tonight the sea will break

and geologics; they bow up

                      its fast and prey on pacifist sands.

their leaf-inflected lauds and burst

                      And God will understand if we don't

into mezzo forte. And from this doorway

                      want to go swimming.

I sing louder. Soon we'll all decrescendo.

The Hill Gods

> *"Meanwhile, the officials of the king of Aram advised him, 'Their gods are gods of the hills. That is why they were too strong for us.'"*
> —1 Kings 20:23

Those gods of the hills, those with carved bark
faces, they spit and mud slithers down like serpents
before the herders' fire. They catch suicidal
stars and howl at the cuticle
moon. From stone-ringed raths they plot
the overthrow of constellations and mountain
ranges. Here in the hills they wear tunics
made of cresting dawn and ringfort
helmets. Their totems and ancestor shrines
are small but full of sincerity. Their deity dependent

on elevation, they climb buttes and ridges
until valleys threaded by rivers need nymphs
and harvest gods. Have you never seen
a salmon swim up-
hill to find the source of all running
water—a spring in the basement of the hill gods?
They all get eaten by cave bears and dire wolves and cooked
by Irish heroes. Even the mud daubers are subject
to parasites. Hill gods long for liberation
but can never cast off the shadow
of ancient glaciers. One day they'll shrug
off the monasteries and tectonic
into vapor, rigid with isosceles.

The hill gods, whose bread doesn't need leaven
to rise, it follows alpine gravity;
the hill gods, who'll never reign beyond
the piedmont; the hill gods, who dance
to bassoon and dulcimer and eat the fruit that sprouts
from the feces of flying foxes; they hate
snow and all things flat. They die and drop
with rain to puddle in abandoned tires
with mosquito larvae. Their death-scent returns
to clouds and we valley dwellers inhale
their resurrection.

As I Went Down to the River to Pray

What druid night is this that stars would light littoral paths over Milky
        Way waters?
Trees swaying like anemone fronds, planet-spinners darting in and out
        of their folds
like clownfish, all around the air hums with the vibration of a million
wings. Tonight, the holy beckons as if it's a person, an entity, a swallow
        dipped

in star water. Tonight, a trout dances on the bank, basking in moonlit
desiccation; tomorrow it will be simply a piece of bark, a boat of
        papyrus, a misshelved
book. But for now its gasping eye sees only the view from above the
        water, entranced by beauty
without refraction. The wind carries burdens too heavy to transport
        and drops them

along the banks. Leaves, feathers, lightning bugs, the shrill of frogs, the
        moment when tonight
becomes tomorrow, all fall like nightjumping paratroopers, the spin of
        rotors fading
overhead. Somewhere to the east everything deepens and cloud-shoals
        swirl around
the beacon. The world will wake and find a dead fish, never bothering
        to search its eyes

for the remnants of nightsky. How long until the drinking gourd is full
        and stars pour
out their tomorrows? All of creation groans with mercy. Not yet.

A Word to St. Damien of Molokai on the Occasion of His Canonization

Your skin falling like coconut
shavings, dandruff
from my dry scalp, the dried-up
salt from the tears of God,
and you just standing there
watching the sea nibble

at the cliffs like a cane rat.
Your outrigger sailing by
torchlight; your tiki grimacing from
numbness; your soil barren and full
of clay and still you tend
to your flock of sheared lambs.

Gloria Patri—these coastal winds
exhale doxology.

Variations on a Theme by the Prophet Joel

"Your old men will dream dreams; your young men will see visions."
—Joel 2:28

Your old men will mow lawns with walrus tusks;
your young men will sow the soil with salt and produce
chemically altered grass that stops growing at three-quarters
of an inch. When your old men lay down

to sleep they'll pretend the stars are the winking
eyes of God; your young men will smear
the thorax-juice of fireflies beneath their eyes,
brightness of pupils on the upper
cheek, optical illusions like a glowing
Death's-head moth, until they stop looking
for the decoy eyes of deity. When your old men walk

the shores they'll pull out maps as brittle
as last year's palm fronds; when your young men kick
through ash-grained beaches they'll mock
the tide's indecision. Your old men will sing

kingfisher songs, rondeaux praising mid-air
snatching; your young men will tattoo their calves
with ink-tipped frog tongues so they can always taste
the flavor of saliva and feel wings fly up
their thighs. One day your old men will close

their eyes and see wax melting off a cuticle
moon; your young men will open
their eyes and see the moon aging, filling,
becoming whole and covered in sores
of light. On that day your young men will grow
old and your old men will die.

Prayer to St. Margaret of Cortona

for Zoe

It's dark, Margaret, darker than
leafy shadows that hide the faces
of the back-alley murdered, the blankness of new
moon sky, the refuge of centipedes on the other side
of moss. It's dark, Margaret, and I'm tempted

to personify everything as crying—the streetlight
parabola on this pavement reeking
of rain, the empty sky, the leaves disconnected
from home, from branch, from blood and life.
It's dark, Margaret, and I am alone beneath the smoldering

of heaven, the blanket-topped
coals. I am trapped, a starfly stuck on unseen contact paper,
a drowning diver staring watery eyes at the lures
of anglerfish. Morning brings no release, only the ability to see
my captivity. It's dark, Margaret. All my prayers to you, bouncing

off, echolocations to navigate by, return
bruised and well-travelled. No miracle tonight—the lamplight
is still artificial, the moon is still in transit, home is still a taunting
definition, tomorrow is still not today. But, Margaret,
I'll tuck myself into the backseat

and dream of noise and distractions and all of the adiaphora
that clutters these meaningless lives. Life is too sparse
without it. It's dark, Margaret. Wink to me tonight,
slice a crescent into the curtains of heaven, let the moon out
and let me in, overturn this rock and I'll scramble

like a light-drunk potato bug. It's dark, Margaret, and I am alone.
Keep me company with your dirty face and streetlight nimbus.
Mother of hoboes, of prostitutes, the insane, the tramps, the orphaned,
the recessioned, the downlucked, the backwrithing beetles,
luminate.

Epilogue

En Ascuas es el Amor

Take these letters and burn them
until the flames become
kingfisher feathers.

Take the ashes and feed them
to the wind until they are carried
off to the tomb of D.B. Cooper.

Find his skull and grind it
until the mortar and pestle
grin like the riverbed in May.

Walk the riverbed in August
until your feet are spotted
like ocelot paws.

Turn your feet inside out
and wear them proudly, veins
leading the traveler into new realms of cartography.

Take those new maps and hold them
up to the sun, write your response
across the heel, send it south toward the bay.

I'll be adrift among the mangroves.
I'll be singing my kingfisher song.
I'll be tending the next fire.

P. S.
───────────────────────────────

When All Endings Look the Same

> *i. On April Fools' Day*
> Soon I'll sit alone on the riverbanks
>   surrounded by the breeze
>   from amphibian tongues.
>   Tonight my company
>   croaks a Hebrew song
>   of liberation and the frog-tide
> begins to wane. How
>   did Yahweh get all the frogs back
>   into the river?

ii. El

    our tide is receding

        darkness spreads

           across these doorways

              and the night smells

                  like lambs' blood

                      and the absence of yeast

The New York Quarterly Foundation, Inc.
New York, New York

Poetry Magazine
Since 1969

Edgy, fresh, groundbreaking, eclectic—voices from all walks of life.

Definitely NOT your mama's poetry magazine!

The *New York Quarterly* has been defining the term contemporary American poetry since its first craft interview with W. H. Auden.

Interviews • Essays • and of course, lots of poems.

www.nyquarterly.org

No contest! That's correct, NYQ Books are NO CONTEST to other small presses because we do not support ourselves through contests. Our books are carefully selected by invitation only, so you know that NYQ Books are produced with the same editorial integrity as the magazine that has brought you the most eclectic contemporary American poetry since 1969.

Books

nyqbooks.org

poetry at the edge™

www.ingramcontent.com/pod-product-compliance
Lightning Source LLC
Chambersburg PA
CBHW031137090426
42738CB00008B/1115